This book belongs to:

_____

FAMILY TREE

The Greatest Gift is Family

PARENT NAME   PARENT NAME

SIBLINGS

GRANDPARENTS   GRANDPARENTS

AUNTS & UNCLES   AUNTS & UNCLES

YOUR STORY
Our Journey to You

How We Found You:

Our Journey To Meet You:

What You Mean To Us:

YOUR FOREVER FAMILY

Love you for always...

MOMMY

DADDY

BABY

All About Mommy

FULL NAME   BIRTHDAY

WHERE I GREW UP

MY FAVORITE CHILDHOOD MEMORIES

MY INTERESTS & HOBBIES

WHAT I WANT YOU TO KNOW ABOUT ME

Love Letter From Mommy

_____

_____

_____

_____

_____

_____

_____

_____

_____

NEVER FORGET...

I'LL LOVE YOU forever I'LL LIKE YOU FOR always AS LONG AS I'M LIVING my Baby YOU'LL BE.

MY DREAM FOR YOU...

All About Daddy

FULL NAME

BIRTHDAY

WHERE I GREW UP

MY FAVORITE CHILDHOOD MEMORIES

MY INTERESTS & HOBBIES

WHAT I WANT YOU TO KNOW ABOUT ME

Love Letter From Daddy

_____

_____

_____

_____

_____

_____

_____

_____

_____

NEVER FORGET...

MY DREAM FOR YOU...

MEMORIES OF YOU
Your First Year Photo Checklist

FIRST YEAR PHOTO CHECKLIST:

Our first day with you

Baby's first bath

First family photo

Baby's hands with ours

Baby & Mommy

Baby's first doctor visit

Baby's first haircut

Learning to crawl

Baby's first time standing

Baby giving kisses

Baby with favorite toy

Baby in nursery

First feeding

Baby's first outfit

Baby & Daddy

Baby with Grandparents

Baby with siblings

Baby sitting up

Baby sleeping

Baby's first birthday party

Getting into mischief!

Baby in the car seat

OTHER PHOTO IDEAS:

MILESTONES
Watching You Grow

Lifts Head:

 Age:

Smiles:

 Age:

Rolls onto Back:

 Age:

Laughs:

 Age:

Grasps Objects:

 Age:

Says Mama:

 Age:

Sleeps Through the Night:

 Age:

Reaches for Objects:

 Age:

Discovers Hands & Feet:

 Age:

Coos & Babbles:

 Age:

First Tooth:

 Age:

Eats Solid Food:

 Age:

Says Dada:

 Age:

Pulls up to standing position:

 Age:

MILESTONES
Watching You Grow

Takes a few steps:

Age:

First word with understanding:

Age:

Turns towards sounds:

Age:

Points to named things:

Age:

Recognizes Family Members

Age:

Kicks a ball:

Age:

Shakes head for yes or no:

Age:

Takes first step unassisted:

Age:

Sits without support:

Age:

Likes to look into mirror:

Age:

Builds block towers:

Age:

Drinks from a cup:

Age:

Watching you grow is our greatest joy...

	Height:	Weight:
1 MONTH		
2 MONTHS		
3 MONTHS		
4 MONTHS		
5 MONTHS		

Watching you grow is our greatest joy...

	Height:	Weight:
6 MONTHS		
7 MONTHS		
8 MONTHS		
9 MONTHS		
10 MONTHS		

Watching you grow is our greatest joy...

	Height:	Weight:
11 MONTHS		
12 MONTHS		
13 MONTHS		
14 MONTHS		
15 MONTHS		

Watching you grow is our greatest joy...

	Height:	Weight:
16 MONTHS		
17 MONTHS		
18 MONTHS		
19 MONTHS		
20 MONTHS		

	Height:	Weight:
21 MONTHS		
22 MONTHS		
23 MONTHS		
24 MONTHS		

Two years of beautiful memories

REFLECTIONS:

You're our greatest gift...

MONTH 1	THOUGHTS

MONTH 2	THOUGHTS

MONTH 3	THOUGHTS

MONTH 4	THOUGHTS

MONTH 5	THOUGHTS

You're our pride & joy...

MONTH 6	THOUGHTS

MONTH 7	THOUGHTS

MONTH 8	THOUGHTS

MONTH 9	THOUGHTS

MONTH 10	THOUGHTS

You're our everything...

MONTH 11	THOUGHTS

MONTH 12	THOUGHTS

Our Favorite Memories

Photos to Remember

1 *Year* *Old* ♡

2 *Year's* *Old* ♡

Photos to Remember

3 *Year's Old* ♡

4 *Year's Old* ♡

YOUR FIRST YEAR
Love You to the Moon & Back

ALL ABOUT YOU

WEIGHT:

HEIGHT:

FAV FOOD:

FAV ACTIVITY:

THE WORLD YOU LIVE IN

TOP SONGS:

HEADLINES:

WORLD LEADERS:

YEARLY MILESTONES

YOUR FAVORITE THINGS

WHAT WE DID TO CELEBRATE

YEAR ONE PHOTO
Your Smile Fills Our Hearts

love
IS
forever

YEAR IN REVIEW

We Never Want to Miss a Thing

SLEEPS SOUNDLY

LIFTS HEAD

PLAYS WITH TOYS

LIFTS UPPER BODY

ROLLS OVER

BEGINS TO TALK

BEGINS TO CRAWL

SITTING UP

YEAR ONE THOUGHTS & FEELINGS

YEAR TWO PHOTO
A Love that Lasts Forever

ALL YOU
need
IS
love

YEAR THREE PHOTO

You're the light of our lives

YEAR FOUR PHOTO

Twinkle twinkle, little star...

YEAR FIVE PHOTO

Mommy's Angel, Daddy's Joy

Photos to Remember

1 *Year Old* ♡

2 *Year's Old* ♡

Photos to Remember

3 Years Old ♡

4 Years Old ♡

Printed in Great Britain
by Amazon